# CONTROLLING INVASIVE SPECIES

Liz Chung

**PowerKiDS**
press.

New York

Published in 2017 by The Rosen Publishing Group, Inc.
29 East 21st Street, New York, NY 10010

First Edition

Editor: Theresa Morlock
Book Design: Reann Nye

Photo Credits: Cover (background), pp. 1–24 (background) jwblinn/Shutterstock.com; cover (map), pp.1–24 Buslik/Shutterstock.com; cover (top) Luís Cerqueira/Moment/ Getty Images; cover (bottom) SSokolov/Shutterstock.com; p.5 (top) photoiconix/ Shutterstock.com; p. 5 (middle) Chris Ison/Shutterstock.com; p. 5 (bottom) 1082492116/Shutterstock.com; p. 6 Sunny Forest/Shutterstock.com; p. 7 KPG_ Payless/Shutterstock.com; p. 9 J.K. York/Shutterstock.com; p. 10 Joe Raedle/ Getty Images News/Getty Images; p. 11 (top) Elliotte Rusty Harold/Shutterstock.com; p. 11 (bottom) Ponpirun/Shutterstock.com; p. 13 (top) Gypsytwitcher/Shutterstock. com; p. 13 (bottom) https://commons.wikimedia.org/wiki/File:Rabbits_Myxomatosis-Trial_WardangIsland_1938.jpg; p. 14 cellistka/Shutterstock.com; p. 15 Heiko Kiera/ Shutterstock.com; p. 16 Janelle Lugge/Shutterstock.com; p. 17 Aitor Gonzalez Frias/ Shutterstock.com; p. 19 AFP/Getty Images; p. 21 JAY DIRECTO/AFP/Getty Images; p. 22 bikeriderlondon/Shutterstock.com.

Cataloging-in-Publication Data

Names: Chung, Liz.
Title: Controlling invasive species / Liz Chung.
Description: New York : PowerKids Press, 2017. | Series: Global guardians | Includes index.
Identifiers: ISBN 9781499427585 (pbk.) | ISBN 9781499429374 (library bound) | ISBN 9781508152736 (6 pack)
Subjects: LCSH: Introduced organisms-Juvenile literature. | Biological invasions-Juvenile literature.
Classification: LCC QH353.C58 2017 | DDC 578.62-d23

Manufactured in China

CPSIA Compliance Information: Batch #BW17PK: For Further Information contact Rosen Publishing, New York, New York at 1-800-237-9932

# CONTENTS

# MAKE WAY FOR INVADERS

Millions of kinds of plants and animals call Earth home. These wonderful creatures live in many different **environments**—from deserts to plains to oceans. All the living organisms in an environment are part of a community of living and nonliving things, called an ecosystem. The plants and animals that naturally live and grow in an ecosystem are called native **species**. "Native" means something belongs in an environment.

A healthy ecosystem has a balance of native plants and animals. They **depend** on each other to survive and keep their ecosystem healthy. Sometimes new species invade, or take over, ecosystems. Invasive species can hurt the species already living there—as well as the ecosystem itself.

## CONSERVATION CLUES

Invasive species are plants and animals that don't naturally live in an area and that can cause a lot of harm to it.

water hyacinth

cane toad

zebra mussels

Do any of these creatures look harmful? Look again—some may be hurting the environment!

# IMPORTANT ROLES

Every creature in an ecosystem is important. Every living thing has a job to do. This is called its niche. Take a pond ecosystem, for example. Plants clean the water. Bugs eat the plants. Bugs are eaten by little fish, which are then eaten by big fish. Everything works well together, and there's enough food for all.

Now imagine how the pond ecosystem would change if an invasive species arrived. Water hyacinths can be invasive plants. They multiply, or increase in numbers, quickly. If water hyacinths aren't controlled, they can take over a pond. They cover the water's surface and block out the sun, which kills other plants.

Water hyacinths are slowly taking over the surface of this pond. What will happen if the plants aren't controlled?

# CRAZY KUDZU

Have you ever heard of weeds? These pesky plants always grow where we don't want them. For this reason, some invasive plants are considered weeds.

Invasive species may spread quickly and use up the sunlight and water that native plants need to grow. Their seeds are often carried by the wind and by animals. Sometimes people are the **culprits**!

Long ago, people brought the kudzu vine to America from Asia because they thought it was beautiful. However, the vines of this plant grow very quickly. As they grow, they kill other plants in their way.

## CONSERVATION CLUES

The kudzu vine is called "the vine that ate the [American] South." Kudzu was introduced to the United States at the Philadelphia Continental Exposition in 1876. Farmers were told kudzu would help stop soil from blowing away, Unfortunately, it took over!

Kudzu climbs up and over anything in its way. It smothers, or covers, native plants. This prevents native plants from getting sunlight and air.

# SMALL, BUT MIGHTY

Even the tiniest bugs can cause big trouble. Red **imported** fire ants are an invasive species. They're small, but their sting can hurt people, pets, and livestock such as cows. Red imported fire ants are native to South America and probably arrived in the United States on ships that traveled between countries.

The northern snakehead fish is native to China, Russia, and Korea, but it's causing big problems in the Potomac River near Washington, D.C. The fish are predators that eat the small fish and frogs that native fish need to survive. Since 2004, they've taken over about 60 miles (96.6 km) of river, and scientists are worried about what damage, or harm, these invaders will cause.

Northern snakehead fish

The red imported fire ant doesn't just hurt animals and plants in its ecosystem. It can hurt people, too.

# SPREADING QUICKLY

Invasive species may spread quickly because they usually don't have natural predators in their new environment, and they may not have to compete for food. The species can grow **unchecked**. That's how the European rabbit became an invasive species in Australia. In 1859, about 24 rabbits were released into the wild. At first nothing **preyed** on them, so the number of rabbits grew quickly. By 1926, Australia had about 10 billion rabbits! They ate many plants, which hurt the soil and the populations of other plant-eating animals.

Many kinds of birds are invasive too, including the common pigeon. They eat farmers' crops and they can carry **diseases** that can make people, animals, and other birds very sick.

## CONSERVATION CLUES

Scientists will sometimes manage invasive species through natural means. They introduce an invasive species' predator or a disease that will kill the species in large numbers. This too can damage the environment.

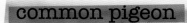

Scientists worry about invasive species that carry diseases. The native species (including people) might not have a way to fight off a sickness if they've never had to before.

rabbits at a watering hole in Australia in the 1930s

# PROBLEMATIC PETS

Ecosystems are very **delicate**, and even our pets can upset the balance. Pets become invasive species if they escape or are let go by their owners. In the wild, dogs and cats survive by eating native plants and animals. These common pets have destroyed ecosystems.

**Exotic** pets can also cause damage if they escape. Sometimes their owners let them go if they become too large or require too much work. The Burmese python is a perfect example. The Florida Everglades is overrun with these powerful snakes. Native animals such as the mangrove fox squirrel are no match for these beasts, which can be up to 23 feet (7 m) long.

yellow anaconda

## CONSERVATION CLUES

Snakes must like Florida! Many nonnative species have been found there, including the common boa, green anaconda, yellow anaconda, and reticulated python.

Burmese pythons **thrive** in Florida. The tropical climate, lack of predators, and undisturbed **habitats** in the Everglades mean the Burmese python population has a good chance of surviving.

# ISLANDS UNDER ATTACK

Island ecosystems are even more at **risk** when invasive species are introduced. Since islands are separated from the mainland, native species don't often come into contact with nonnative species. When they do, the members of the native species often can't **protect** themselves.

Brown tree snakes arrived on the island of Guam in the 1950s. The snakes multiplied quickly and killed many native birds, lizards, and other small animals. Unfortunately, the snakes didn't have any predators there, which allowed them to thrive.

Velvet trees from South America have taken over forests in Tahiti and Hawaii. The trees' large leaves block out the sunlight, meaning plants can't grow underneath them. Without those plants, soil wears away, and the ecosystems suffer.

brown tree snake

Invasive species are a problem for islands. The invaders often have no natural predators and no competition! Unfortunately, humans are usually responsible for bringing invasive species to islands.

17

# DEALING WITH THE PROBLEM

It's our job to deal with invasive species when they arrive in our ecosystems. People use several methods to control invasive species. One method is biocontrol. This is when people place predators of an invasive species in an ecosystem. If it works, the predators help control the invader's population. Sometimes people use chemicals to drive invasive species away, but this can hurt other creatures in the ecosystem too.

Live capture is a way to control the problem without hurting any species, invasive or not. This method allows people to remove invasive plants and animals without killing them.

## CONSERVATION CLUES

People can help control zebra mussels, an invasive species that threatens many ecosystems. Boaters should always check their boat after it comes out of the water to make sure zebra mussels aren't attached. This way, they can't be introduced anywhere else when the boat goes back in the water.

zebra
mussels

Zebra mussels, which are native to eastern Europe, invaded Lake Ontario and the rest of the Great Lakes. Once captured, invasive species can be returned to their natural home or placed in a controlled environment.

# WE NEED NATIVE SPECIES

After an invasive species is removed from an area, it's important to help the native species it has driven out or hurt. After all, the ecosystem needs its native plant and animal species. They each have a job to do to keep the ecosystem balanced.

Caring for native species protects biodiversity. Biodiversity is having many different types of species living together in an ecosystem. Invasive species can harm biodiversity, which also affects nonliving things such as soil and water. Planting native plants and reintroducing native animals can make all the parts of an ecosystem healthy once again.

## CONSERVATION CLUES

Reintroduction is putting members of a species back into a place where that species once lived. These baby turtles in the Philippines are hatched in protected nurseries and returned to their natural home.

Reintroduction programs help animals return to where they should be—their natural home. Check with zoos and animal protection groups in your area to see how you can get involved!

How can you help control invasive species? Before adding a new plant to your garden, check to make sure that it belongs in your environment. If it seems exotic or unusual, you may want to plant something else.

Another way to help is to join a group that removes invasive species and plants native ones. Never release a pet into the wild. If you can't care for it, find it a new home. Think carefully before buying an exotic pet. There are many ways you can help control invasive species. The first step is learning about them!

# GLOSSARY

**culprit:** The cause of a problem.

**delicate:** Easily broken or harmed.

**depend:** To need.

**disease:** Sickness.

**environment:** The natural surroundings of a person, plant, or animal.

**exotic:** From another country or place.

**habitat:** The natural home for plants, animals, and other living things.

**imported:** Brought into an area from somewhere else.

**prey:** To hunt for food.

**protect:** To keep safe.

**risk:** The chance of danger.

**species:** A group of plants or animals that are all the same kind.

**thrive:** To grow or live successfully.

**unchecked:** Not controlled.

# INDEX

# WEBSITES

Due to the changing nature of Internet links, PowerKids Press has developed an online list of websites related to the subject of this book. This site is updated regularly. Please use this link to access the list: www.powerkidslinks.com/glob/inva